The Complete Plant Based Diet for Beginners

1000 Days Healthy Diet Recipes and 4 Weeks Meal Plan to Build Your Endurance & Strength

Delois Townsend

Table of Contents

Introduction 5
    What is the Plant Based Diet? 6
    Why go Vegan? 6

Breakfast Recipes 8
    Delicious Baked Oatmeal 8
    Perfect Vegetable Frittata 9
    Spinach Tomato Tofu Scramble 10
    Breakfast Potatoes 11
    Banana Peanut Butter Oatmeal 12
    Healthy Pumpkin Oatmeal 13
    Chia Blackberry Pudding 14
    Quinoa Rice Pudding 15
    Sweet Chia Mango Pudding 16
    Pumpkin Quinoa Porridge 17

Smoothies Recipes 18
    Healthy Green Smoothie 18
    Watermelon Strawberry Smoothie 19
    Gluten-free Berry Smoothie 20
    Blueberry Pineapple Smoothie 21
    Perfect Apple Cinnamon Smoothie 22
    Healthy Dragon Fruit Smoothie 23
    Banana Peanut Butter Smoothie 24
    Cinnamon Apple Oat Smoothie 25

Snacks Recipes 26
    Roasted Chickpeas 26
    Crispy Tofu 27
    Roasted Nuts 28
    Savory Sweet Potato Bites 29
    Air Fryer Walnuts 30
    Easy Energy Bites 31
    Baked Okra 32
    Cauliflower Zucchini Fritters 33

Salads and Sides Recipes 34
    Corn Black Bean Avocado Salad 34
    Healthy Apple Walnut Salad 35
    Gluten-free Broccoli Salad 36
    Cucumber Pineapple Salad 37
    Protein Packed Chickpea Salad 38
    Mango Avocado Salad 39
    Tasty Baked Cabbage 40
    Roasted Brussels Sprouts 41

Dips and Sauces Recipes 42
    Flavorful Tzatziki 42
    Sun-dried Tomato Dip 43
    Roasted Pepper Dip 44
    Easy White Bean Dip 45

Peanut Sauce 46

Tahini Sauce 47

Lunch Recipes 48

Coconut Pumpkin Soup 48

Garlic Basil Tomato Soup 49

Cauliflower Carrot Soup 50

Cauliflower Spinach Rice 51

Basil Zucchini Noodles 52

Sautéed Asparagus & Mushrooms 53

Simple Eggplant Adobo 54

Sautéed Spinach 55

Lemon Garlic Kale 56

Sautéed Veggies 57

Zucchini Spinach Noodles 58

Spinach Broccoli Curry 59

Delicious Vegetable Curry 60

Stir Fried Carrots & Cabbage 61

Zucchini Carrot Noodles 62

Dinner Recipes 63

Lentil Tomato Soup 63

Flavorful Quinoa Salad 64

Sweet Potato Lentil Stew 65

Quinoa Bean Chili 66

Black Beans Rice 67

Spanish Rice & Beans 68

Easy Spanish Quinoa 69

Healthy Lentil Rice 70

Mushroom Garlic Quinoa 71

Brown Rice Broccoli Casserole 72

Mushroom Barley Soup 73

Nutritious Lentil Stew 74

Black Bean Chili 75

Barley Spinach Risotto 76

Delicious Pumpkin Risotto 77

Desserts Recipes 78

Chia Chocó Pudding 78

Choco Peanut Butter Muffins 79

Quick Kiwi Popsicle 80

Baked Apple 81

Easy Lemon Popsicles 82

Easy Strawberry Sorbet 83

Blueberry Popsicles 84

Strawberry Cobbler 85

Chocolate Brownies 86

Lemon Cupcakes 87

30-Day Meal Plan 88

Conclusion 91

Introduction

The plant-based diet is one of the most popular diets nowadays. It's not just a diet plan but it also changes your eating habits towards healthy and nutritious food. These foods are rich in fibres, vitamins, minerals, and antioxidants. Plant based foods are available in many varieties which means you can find lots of different types of recipes on a plant-based diet. The diet restricts animal-based foods and ingredients such as meat, fish, poultry, honey, and dairy products. The plant-based diet helps to make your body healthy and stronger to resist different types of chronic diseases. It improves your physical health as well as mental health.

In this cookbook, we will talk about what exactly the plant-based diet is and why we go with this diet plan. There are many reasons to adopt a vegetarian diet. Some of the main reasons are for your health, environment, and animals have been discussed in this book. If you are a beginner then this book would help with your vegan diet journey.

This cookbook contains 80 healthy and delicious plant-based diet recipes that come under different categories like breakfast, smoothies, snacks, salads and sides, dips and sauces, lunch, dinner, and desserts. The recipes written in this book are unique and written into an easily understandable form. All the recipes start with their preparation and cooking time followed by step-by-step cooking instructions. At the end of each recipe, nutritional value information is written. The nutritional value information will help to keep track of daily calorie intake. There are various books available in the market on this topic thanks for choosing my cookbook. I hope you love and enjoy all the plant-based food recipes written in this book.

What is the Plant Based Diet?

The plant-based diet is one of the most popular diet plans mainly focused on eating plant-based foods only. Plant based food includes minimally processed foods such as vegetables, fruits, whole grains, legumes, herbs, seeds, and nuts. The diet eliminates animal products such as meat, beef, fish, poultry, eggs, honey, and dairy products. It is not just an ordinary diet plan because it changes your eating habit towards healthy and nutritious food eating. There are a huge variety of plant-based foods are available in this category. The daily consumption of plant-based food will help to reduce the harmful effect of different chronic diseases. It also helps to improve your mental health, reduce the chances of heart-related diseases, controls your blood pressure and type-2 diabetes. Most of the studies conducted over a plant-based diet also proves that the diet helps to reduce depression and also improves your physical as well as mental health.

The diet avoids highly processed foods but allows consuming lightly processed foods. There are healthy alternatives available in plant-based food instead of animal-based foods such as cashew milk instead of cow milk, scrambled eggs are replaced with tofu scramble, and replace pulled pork with shredded jackfruit. The plant-based diet is healthy when they are balanced with essential vitamins and nutrients. The well-balanced plant-based diet mainly focuses on fresh fruits, vegetables, whole grains, legumes, nuts, seeds, and herbs. The plants are rich in nutrients, vitamins, and minerals that also help to boost your energy level. The plant-based diet is cholesterol-free and low in saturated fats also rich in fibre, vitamins, and minerals. It also consists of antioxidant properties and the best source of healthy protein and fats.

Why go Vegan?

A vegan does not allow the consumption meat, beef, fish, poultry, eggs, honey, dairy products, and the product derived from any animal. The vegan diet allows only plant-based foods which are packed full of vitamins, minerals, and fibre. The higher intake of vegan foods and a lower intake of animal foods helps to reduce the risk of heart-related disease. There are many reasons to go with a vegan diet or a plant-based diet. Some of the reasons are related to the environment, health, animals, and more.

1. Environment: Going with a vegan diet is one of the biggest things to do to reduce your environmental foot-marks. When you are following a vegan diet, it means that you are producing about 50% less carbon dioxide compared to animal-based food eaters. The Food and Agriculture Organization of the United Nations states that animal agriculture is one of the causes of water pollution. In meat production there is a large amount of grain feed required which leads to deforestation. Animal agriculture produces lots of methane gas which is responsible for the release of 18% of the greenhouse gas effect worldwide. A vegan diet is one of the biggest ways to reduce the greenhouse effect, save water and land.

2. Animals: Animal cruelty is one of the biggest and strongest reasons to adopt a vegan lifestyle. Like human beings, all other animals also feel pain, fear, pleasure, and family love. Most of the animals raised for food have a terrible and torturous life. These animals are living their short life in a factory or farm in a congested place where they cannot move properly and they all lack fresh air. To stop animal cruelty, you need to keep animals away from your kitchen and adopt a natural and healthy vegan lifestyle.

3. Health: Going vegan is one of the healthy choices because you are eating more plant based food. The vegan diet provides all essential vitamins, minerals, and antioxidants to your body. It helps to reduce the risk of cardiovascular disease, get rid of obesity, metabolic syndrome, control blood pressure and type-2 diabetes, and is also effective in cancers. Plant based foods are very effective when it comes to weight loss.

Breakfast Recipes

Delicious Baked Oatmeal

Prep Time: 10 minutes

Cook Time: 40 minutes

Serves: 4

Ingredients:

- 2 cups gluten-free rolled oats
- ⅓ cup peanuts
- ¼ cup chocolate chips
- ⅓ cup peanut butter
- ½ cup maple syrup
- 1½ tsp vanilla extract
- 1½ cups almond milk
- 1 tsp baking powder
- 1 tbsp ground flax seeds
- ½ tsp sea salt

Preparation:

1. Preheat the oven to 350 degrees F.
2. Line 9*9-inch baking pan with parchment paper and set aside.
3. In a bowl, mix oats, baking powder, ground flax seeds, and salt.
4. In a separate mixing bowl, mix together almond milk, peanuts, chocolate chips, peanut butter, maple syrup, and vanilla.
5. Pour almond milk mixture into the oat mixture and mix until well combined.
6. Pour oat mixture into the greased baking pan and bake in preheated oven for 40 minutes.
7. Serve and enjoy.

Serving Suggestion: Slice and serve with some plant-based milk

Variation Tip: You can use chia seeds instead of flax seeds

Nutritional Information Per Serving:

Calories 534 | Fat 24.9g | Sodium 416mg | Carbs 67.9g | Fiber 7.6g | Sugar 32.6g | Protein 15g

Perfect Vegetable Frittata

Prep Time: 10 minutes

Cook Time: 50 minutes

Serves: 6

Ingredients:

- 2 medium potatoes, peel & dice
- ½ cup cherry tomatoes halved
- ½ tsp garlic, minced
- 1 zucchini, diced
- 1 bell pepper, diced
- 1 small onion, diced
- 1 tbsp olive oil
- 1/8 tsp black pepper
- ¼ tsp turmeric
- ½ tsp garlic powder
- 1½ tsp dried thyme
- 1 tsp mustard
- 2 tbsp nutritional yeast
- 2 tsp cornstarch
- ¼ cup unsweetened almond milk
- 16 oz silken tofu, drained
- ½ tsp salt

Preparation:

1. Preheat the oven to 375 degrees F.
2. Heat oil in a pan over medium heat.
3. Add potatoes to the pan and sauté for 5 minutes. Add onion and sauté for 5 minutes.
4. Add garlic, zucchini, and bell pepper, and sauté until softened. Add cherry tomatoes and cook for a minute. Season with pepper and salt.
5. Add tofu, almond milk, cornstarch, nutritional yeast, mustard, thyme, garlic powder, turmeric, pepper, and salt into the blender and blend until smooth.
6. Add sautéed vegetables and tofu mixture into a greased 9-inch pie pan and spread evenly.
7. Bake in preheated oven for 35-45 minutes.
8. Remove from oven and let it cool for 10 minutes.
9. Slice and serve.

Serving Suggestion: Serve the frittata with sliced avocado

Variation Tip: You can use arrowroot flour or tapioca flour instead of cornstarch

Nutritional Information Per Serving:

Calories 156 | Fat 5.1g | Sodium 240mg | Carbs 20.2g | Fiber 3.9g | Sugar 4.3g | Protein 9g

Spinach Tomato Tofu Scramble

Prep Time: 10 minutes

Cook Time: 15 minutes

Serves: 4

Ingredients:

- 14 oz firm tofu, drained & crumbled
- 3 cups fresh baby spinach
- ¾ cup cherry tomatoes halved
- 3 tbsp nutritional yeast
- ¼ tsp onion powder
- ½ tsp garlic powder
- ¼ tsp black pepper
- ¼ tsp paprika
- ½ tsp turmeric
- 2 tbsp lemon juice
- 2 tbsp tahini
- 1 tbsp olive oil
- ¾ tsp salt

Preparation:

1. Heat oil in a pan over medium-high heat.
2. Add tofu, tahini, turmeric, lemon juice, and salt into the pan and stir until well combined.
3. Add nutritional yeast, onion powder, garlic powder, black pepper, and paprika, and stir for 5 minutes.
4. Add spinach and tomatoes, cover, and steam for 3-5 minutes or until spinach is wilted.
5. Remove lid and stir well and cook for 3-5 minutes more.

Serving Suggestion: Serve tofu scramble with avocado and toast

Variation Tip: Add chopped mushrooms and kale to the tofu scramble

Nutritional Information Per Serving:

Calories 187 | Fat 12.4g |Sodium 484mg | Carbs 9.7g | Fiber 4.6g | Sugar 1.9g | Protein 14g

Breakfast Potatoes

Prep Time: 10 minutes

Cook Time: 40 minutes

Serves: 4

Ingredients:

- 5 cups red potatoes, chopped
- ½ tsp old bay seasoning
- 1 tsp garlic powder
- 1 tsp paprika
- 3 tbsp olive oil
- 1 bell pepper, diced
- 1 tbsp garlic, minced
- 1 onion, chopped
- ¼ tsp pepper
- 1 tsp sea salt

Preparation:

1. Preheat the oven to 400 degrees F.
2. In a large mixing bowl, add potatoes, old bay seasoning, garlic powder, paprika, oil, bell pepper, garlic, onion, pepper, and salt and toss until well coated.
3. Add potato mixture into a baking dish and bake in preheated oven for 30 minutes.
4. Turn heat to 425 degrees F and bake potatoes for 10-15 minutes more.

Serving Suggestion: Serve potatoes with ketchup

Variation Tip: You can use Yukon gold potatoes instead of red potatoes

Nutritional Information Per Serving:

Calories 249 | Fat 11g | Sodium 562mg | Carbs 36.2g | Fiber 4.5g | Sugar 4.8g | Protein 4.5g

Banana Peanut Butter Oatmeal

Prep Time: 10 minutes

Cook Time: 30 minutes

Serves: 6

Ingredients:

- 2 cups old-fashioned oats
- 1 tsp vanilla extract
- 1 tbsp ground flaxseed
- 2 tbsp maple syrup
- ¼ cup creamy peanut butter
- 1½ cups unsweetened almond milk
- 2 ripe bananas
- 1 tsp baking powder
- 1 tsp cinnamon
- ¼ tsp salt

Preparation:

1. Preheat the oven to 375 degrees F.
2. Add oats, baking powder, cinnamon, and salt into the baking dish.
3. In a large bowl, mash the bananas, then add vanilla, flaxseed, maple syrup, peanut butter, and milk. Allow to sit for 5 minutes.
4. Add banana mixture over oat mixture and stir to combine.
5. Bake for 30-35 minutes. Remove baking dish from oven and allow to cool for 5 minutes.

Serving Suggestion: Serve with banana slices.

Variation Tip: Don't use maple syrup if you want it to be sugar-free

Nutritional Information Per Serving:

Calories 353 | Fat 13.2g |Sodium 292mg | Carbs 52.8g | Fiber 7.7g | Sugar 15.9g | Protein 10.4g

Healthy Pumpkin Oatmeal

Prep Time: 10 minutes

Cook Time: 5 minutes

Serves: 2

Ingredients:

- 1 cup old fashioned oats
- 1½ cups water
- ¼ cup unsweetened almond milk
- 1 tsp pumpkin pie spice
- ½ cup pumpkin puree
- Pinch of salt

Preparation:

1. Add oats, water, milk, pumpkin pie spice, pumpkin puree, and salt into the saucepan and bring to boil.
2. Turn heat to low and simmer for 3-5 minutes.
3. Remove saucepan from heat and allow to sit for 3-5 minutes.

Serving Suggestion: Add oatmeal in the serving bowl, drizzle with maple syrup and top with pecans

Variation Tip: You can use any non-dairy milk

Nutritional Information Per Serving:

Calories 341 | Fat 5.9g | Sodium 109mg | Carbs 59.5g | Fiber 9.9g | Sugar 4.2g | Protein 10.9g

Chia Blackberry Pudding

Prep Time: 5 minutes

Cook Time: 5 minutes

Serves: 4

Ingredients:

- ¼ cup almonds, toasted & sliced
- 1 tbsp shredded coconut
- 2 tbsp honey
- ½ cup coconut yogurt
- 1 cup unsweetened almond milk
- 3 tbsp chia seeds
- ½ cup fresh blackberries

Preparation:

1. Add blackberries into the mixing bowl and mash using a fork.
2. Add remaining ingredients except for sliced almonds into the mashed blackberries and mix well.
3. Cover bowl and place in refrigerator overnight.

Serving Suggestion: Top with sliced almonds and serve

Variation Tip: Add coconut milk instead of almond milk

Nutritional Information Per Serving:

Calories 136 | Fat 6.5g | Sodium 67mg | Carbs 15.6g | Fiber 2.1g | Sugar 12g | Protein 4.7g

Quinoa Rice Pudding

Prep Time: 10 minutes

Cook Time: 15 minutes

Serves: 6

Ingredients:

- 2 cups cooked quinoa
- 1 tsp cinnamon
- 1½ tsp vanilla extract
- 3 cups cooked brown rice
- 2 tbsp maple syrup
- 13.5 oz coconut milk
- 2½ cups unsweetened almond milk
- 1 ripe banana, mashed
- ¼ tsp salt

Preparation:

1. Add maple syrup, coconut milk, almond milk, banana, and salt into the saucepan and bring to simmer.
2. Add quinoa and rice stir well and simmer until pudding is thickened and creamy about 10 minutes.
3. Remove saucepan from heat and add vanilla and cinnamon. Stir well.

Serving Suggestion: Top with chopped nuts and toasted coconut and serve

Variation Tip: Add almond extract which makes this pudding irresistible

Nutritional Information Per Serving:

Calories 476 | Fat 20.2g |Sodium 198mg | Carbs 66g | Fiber 7.6g | Sugar 10.5g | Protein 11g

Sweet Chia Mango Pudding

Prep Time: 5 minutes

Cook Time: 5 minutes

Serves: 4

Ingredients:

- ¼ cup maple syrup
- 2 cups coconut milk
- ½ cup chia seeds
- 2 fresh mangos, peel & chopped

Preparation:

1. Add mangos into the blender and blend until smooth.
2. In a mixing bowl, add mango puree, maple syrup, coconut milk, and chia seeds and stir well.
3. Cover bowl and place in refrigerator for 15 minutes.
4. Stir pudding after 15 minutes and place again in the refrigerator for 15 minutes.

Serving Suggestion: Spoon pudding into the serving glasses and top with chopped mangos and serve

Variation Tip: You can use mango pulp instead of fresh mangos

Nutritional Information Per Serving:

Calories 497 | Fat 33.9g |Sodium 21mg | Carbs 48g | Fiber 5.3g | Sugar 38.7g | Protein 7.2g

Pumpkin Quinoa Porridge

Prep Time: 10 minutes

Cook Time: 18 minutes

Serves: 5

Ingredients:

- 1½ cups uncooked quinoa, rinsed
- 4 tbsp maple syrup
- 1 tsp cinnamon
- ⅓ cup shredded coconut
- ⅓ cup coconut milk
- 1½ cups pumpkin puree
- 8 oz water
- 12 oz almond milk

Preparation:

1. Add almond milk and water into the medium pot and bring to boil. Add quinoa and stir well and cook over medium-low heat.
2. After 8-10 minutes add pumpkin puree and stir well. Cover again and cook until quinoa is fluffy (about 10 minutes).
3. Remove the pot from heat. Add coconut milk and spices and stir well.
4. Stir in maple syrup and shredded coconut.

Serving Suggestion: Top with chopped nuts and granola and serve

Variation Tip: To make it sweeter you can add coconut sugar

Nutritional Information Per Serving:

Calories 322 | Fat 9.9g | Sodium 62mg | Carbs 52g | Fiber 7g | Sugar 12.8g | Protein 8.9g

Smoothies Recipes

Healthy Green Smoothie

Prep Time: 5 minutes

Cook Time: 5 minutes

Serves: 2

Ingredients:

- 1 cup unsweetened almond milk
- ¼ cup orange juice
- 2 tbsp hemp seeds
- 2 cups baby spinach
- 1 cup frozen mango
- 1 banana, peel

Preparation:

1. Add all the ingredients into the blender and blend until smooth and creamy.

Serving Suggestion: Pour smoothie into the serving glasses and squeeze with lemon juice and serve

Variation Tip: Add pineapple instead of mango

Nutritional Information Per Serving:

Calories 153 | Fat 2.1g |Sodium 115mg | Carbs 34.8g | Fiber 4.1g | Sugar 24g | Protein 2.2g

Watermelon Strawberry Smoothie

Prep Time: 5 minutes

Cook Time: 5 minutes

Serves: 2

Ingredients:

- 4 cups watermelon, seedless & chopped
- 1 tbsp hemp seeds
- ¾ cup cashew yogurt
- 1 cup frozen strawberries

Preparation:

1. Add all the ingredients into the blender and blend until smooth.

Serving Suggestion: Serve immediately

Variation Tip: You can use any frozen berry instead of strawberries

Nutritional Information Per Serving:

Calories 116 | Fat 0.4g | Sodium 4mg | Carbs 29.4g | Fiber 2.7g | Sugar 23.1g | Protein 1.8g

Gluten-free Berry Smoothie

Prep Time: 5 minutes

Cook Time: 5 minutes

Serves: 2

Ingredients:

- 1 cup water
- 1 cup coconut yogurt
- 1 cup frozen strawberries
- ½ cup frozen raspberries
- ½ cup frozen blueberries
- 1 pear, core & diced
- 1 apple, core & diced

Preparation:

1. Add all the ingredients into the blender and blend until smooth.

Serving Suggestion: Pour smoothie into the serving glasses and top with mint leaves and serve

Variation Tip: Add cashew yogurt instead of coconut yogurt

Nutritional Information Per Serving:

Calories 263 | Fat 2.5g | Sodium 6mg | Carbs 60.9g | Fiber 10g | Sugar 46.6g | Protein 3.2g

Blueberry Pineapple Smoothie

Prep Time: 5 minutes

Cook Time: 5 minutes

Serves: 2

Ingredients:

- 1 cup unsweetened almond milk
- 1 tbsp chia seeds
- 1 ripe banana
- 1 handful blueberries
- 1 cup frozen pineapple chunks

Preparation:

1. Add all the ingredients into the blender and blend until smooth.

Serving Suggestion: Top with chia seeds and serve

Variation Tip: You can use any non-dairy milk instead of almond milk

Nutritional Information Per Serving:

Calories 195 | Fat 3.2g | Sodium 93mg | Carbs 42.4g | Fiber 3.4g | Sugar 33.1g | Protein 2.4g

Perfect Apple Cinnamon Smoothie

Prep Time: 5 minutes

Cook Time: 5 minutes

Serves: 2

Ingredients:

- 2 apples, core & diced
- ½ cup ice cubes
- ½ tsp cinnamon
- 1 tsp vanilla
- 1 date, pitted
- 2 tbsp chia seeds
- 2 tbsp hemp hearts
- 2 tbsp almond butter
- ⅓ cup rolled oats
- 1½ cups unsweetened almond milk

Preparation:

1. Add all the ingredients into the blender and blend until smooth.

Serving Suggestion: Sprinkle cinnamon on top and serve.

Variation Tip: Use any non-dairy milk instead of almond milk.

Nutritional Information Per Serving:

Calories 406 | Fat 19.6g | Sodium 141mg | Carbs 50.9g | Fiber 10.8g | Sugar 27g | Protein 11.5g

Cinnamon Apple Oat Smoothie

Prep Time: 5 minutes

Cook Time: 5 minutes

Serves: 1

Ingredients:

- 1 medium apple, peel, core & diced
- ½ cup oat milk
- ¼ tsp cinnamon
- 1 tbsp almond butter
- ¼ cup rolled oats

Preparation:

1. Add all ingredients into the blender and blend until smooth.

Serving Suggestion: Sprinkle with cinnamon and serve

Variation Tip: You can use cashew butter instead of almond butter

Nutritional Information Per Serving:

Calories 358 | Fat 12g |Sodium 57mg | Carbs 60.1g | Fiber 10.4g | Sugar 33.6g | Protein 8.7g

Snacks Recipes

Roasted Chickpeas

Prep Time: 5 minutes

Cook Time: 45 minutes

Serves: 4

Ingredients:

- 14 oz can chickpeas, drained
- ¼ tsp curry powder
- ½ tsp paprika
- ¼ tsp garlic powder
- ¼ tsp ground cumin
- ¼ tsp chili powder
- Pinch of salt

Preparation:

1. Preheat the oven to 375 degrees F.
2. Spread chickpeas on a baking sheet and roast in the oven for 35-45 minutes. Stir 1-2 times.
3. In a mixing bowl, add spices and mix well.
4. Spray roasted chickpeas with cooking spray and add to the mixing bowl. Toss chickpeas until well coated with the spices.

Serving Suggestion: Serve immediately for crunchiness

Variation Tip: You can add your choice of spices

Nutritional Information Per Serving:

Calories 121 | Fat 1.2g |Sodium 337mg | Carbs 22.9g | Fiber 4.6g | Sugar 0.1g | Protein 5g

Crispy Tofu

Prep Time: 10 minutes

Cook Time: 13 minutes

Serves: 4

Ingredients:

- 12 oz extra-firm tofu, press & cut into ½-inch cubes
- ½ tsp black pepper
- 1 tsp garlic powder
- 1 tsp onion powder
- 1 tsp paprika
- 2 tsp cornstarch
- 1 tbsp olive oil
- ½ tsp salt

Preparation:

1. Preheat the oven to 390 degrees F.
2. Add tofu and remaining ingredients into the mixing bowl and toss until well coated.
3. Add tofu to a baking pan and bake for 13 minutes. Shake the after every 5 minutes.

Serving Suggestion: Serve immediately

Variation Tip: Add peanut oil or vegetable oil instead of olive oil

Nutritional Information Per Serving:

Calories 119 | Fat 8.6g | Sodium 298mg | Carbs 4.4g | Fiber 0.7g | Sugar 0.9g | Protein 8.7g

Roasted Nuts

Prep Time: 5 minutes

Cook Time: 15 minutes

Serves: 12

Ingredients:

- ½ cup pecan halves
- ½ cup hazelnuts
- 1 cup cashews
- 1 cup almonds
- ¼ tsp cayenne
- ¼ tsp black pepper
- ½ tsp garlic powder
- 1 tbsp coconut sugar
- 2 tbsp fresh rosemary, chopped
- 2 tbsp maple syrup
- 1 tsp salt

Preparation:

1. Preheat the oven to 325 degrees F.
2. Line baking sheet with parchment paper and set aside.
3. Add pecans, hazelnuts, cashews, almonds, and remaining ingredients into the mixing bowl and toss well.
4. Spread nuts onto the prepared baking sheet and roast in preheated oven for 12-15 minutes. Stir after every 5 minutes.

Serving Suggestion: Allow to cool completely then serve

Variation Tip: You can add brown sugar instead of coconut sugar

Nutritional Information Per Serving:

Calories 177 | Fat 14.9g |Sodium 196mg | Carbs 9.3g | Fiber 2.4g | Sugar 3.2g | Protein 4.5g

Savory Sweet Potato Bites

Prep Time: 10 minutes

Cook Time: 45 minutes

Serves: 6

Ingredients:

- 2 lbs. sweet potatoes, peel and cut into ½-inch cubes
- ½ tsp chili powder
- ½ tsp cinnamon
- 2 tbsp olive oil
- ½ tsp onion powder
- ½ tsp garlic powder
- Pepper
- Salt

Preparation:

1. Preheat the oven to 400 degrees F.
2. Line baking sheet with parchment paper and set aside.
3. Add sweet potatoes and remaining ingredients into the mixing bowl and toss until well coated.
4. Spread sweet potatoes onto the baking sheet and roast for 40-45 minutes. Stir halfway through.

Serving Suggestion: Allow to cool completely then serve

Variation Tip: Add paprika for more spiciness

Nutritional Information Per Serving:

Calories 221 | Fat 5g | Sodium 43mg | Carbs 42.8g | Fiber 6.4g | Sugar 0.9g | Protein 2.4g

Air Fryer Walnuts

Prep Time: 5 minutes.

Cook Time: 5 minutes.

Serves: 6

Ingredients:

- 2 cups walnuts
- ¼ tsp chili powder
- 1 tsp olive oil
- Pepper
- Salt

Preparation:

1. Add walnuts, chili powder, oil, pepper, and salt into the mixing bowl and toss well.
2. Add walnuts into the air fryer basket and air fry at 320 degrees F for 5 minutes.

Serving Suggestion: Allow to cool completely then serve

Variation Tip: You can use vegetable oil instead of olive oil

Nutritional Information Per Serving:

Calories 265 | Fat 25.4g |Sodium 29mg | Carbs 4.2g | Fiber 2.9g | Sugar 0.5g | Protein 10g

Easy Energy Bites

Prep Time: 10 minutes

Cook Time: 10 minutes

Serves: 15

Ingredients:

- ¼ cup shredded coconut
- 1 cup rolled oats
- ¼ cup chocolate chips
- ½ tsp vanilla
- 2 tbsp maple syrup
- ½ cup peanut butter, creamy

Preparation:

1. Add all ingredients into the bowl and mix until well combined.
2. Take a tablespoon of dough and make a small ball.
3. Place balls onto a parchment-lined plate and place in refrigerator.

Serving Suggestion: Serve energy bites once chilled

Variation Tip: You can also use gluten-free oats instead of rolled oats

Nutritional Information Per Serving:

Calories 98 | Fat 6g | Sodium 43mg | Carbs 9.1g | Fiber 1.3g | Sugar 4g | Protein 3.1g

Baked Okra

Prep Time: 10 minutes

Cook Time: 15 minutes

Serves: 4

Ingredients:

- 1 lb. fresh okra, cut into ¾-inch pieces
- 2 tbsp olive oil
- 1 tsp paprika
- ¼ tsp chili powder
- Salt

Preparation:

1. Preheat the oven to 390 degrees F.
2. Add okra, paprika, chili powder, olive oil, and salt into the bowl and toss well.
3. Spread okra onto the baking sheet and bake in preheated oven for 15 minutes.

Serving Suggestion: Allow to cool completely then serve

Variation Tip: You can use vegetable oil instead of olive oil

Nutritional Information Per Serving:

Calories 107 | Fat 7.3g |Sodium 49mg | Carbs 8.8g | Fiber 3.9g | Sugar 1.7g | Protein 2.3g

Cauliflower Zucchini Fritters

Prep Time: 10 minutes

Cook Time: 8 minutes

Serves: 4

Ingredients:

- 2 medium zucchinis, grated and squeezed
- 3 cups cauliflower rice
- 1 tbsp olive oil
- ¼ cup coconut flour
- ½ tsp sea salt

Preparation:

1. Add all the ingredients except for the oil into a bowl and mix until well combined.
2. Heat oil in a pan over medium heat.
3. Make small patties from the mixture and place on the hot pan and cook for 3-4 minutes on each side or until lightly brown from both sides.

Serving Suggestion: Serve fritters with ketchup

Variation Tip: You can use vegetable oil instead of olive oil

Nutritional Information Per Serving:

Calories 94 | Fat 4.5g |Sodium 266mg | Carbs 12.3g | Fiber 6g | Sugar 3.5g | Protein 3.7g

Salads and Sides Recipes

Corn Black Bean Avocado Salad

Prep Time: 10 minutes

Cook Time: 10 minutes

Serves: 10

Ingredients:

- 30 oz can black beans, drained & rinsed
- ½ tsp ground cumin
- 2 tbsp maple syrup
- 3 lime juice
- ½ cup fresh cilantro, minced
- 4 medium tomatoes, chopped
- 2 avocados, chopped
- 16 oz frozen corn
- ¾ tsp salt

Preparation:

1. In a mixing bowl, add black beans, tomatoes, avocados, corn, and cilantro and mix well.
2. In a small bowl, whisk lime juice, cumin, maple syrup, and salt.
3. Drizzle dressing over salad and toss well.

Serving Suggestion: Serve salad with tortilla chips

Variation Tip: Add cooked black beans instead of can beans.

Nutritional Information Per Serving:

Calories 392 | Fat 11.2g | Sodium 531mg | Carbs 69.6g | Fiber 14g | Sugar 12.5g | Protein 13.8g

Healthy Apple Walnut Salad

Prep Time: 10 minutes

Cook Time: 5 minutes

Serves: 4

Ingredients:

- 1 apple, diced
- ½ cup walnuts, chopped
- ½ cup fresh parsley, chopped
- 13.5 oz can chickpeas, rinsed & drained
- 2 celery stalks, diced
- 1 cup red cabbage, shredded

For dressing:

- 1 tbsp maple syrup
- 1 tbsp Dijon mustard
- 2 tbsp apple cider vinegar
- 2 tbsp olive oil

Preparation:

1. Add apple, walnuts, parsley, chickpeas, celery, and cabbage in a large bowl and mix well.
2. In a small bowl, whisk together all dressing ingredients.
3. Pour dressing over salad and toss well.

Serving Suggestion: Serve immediately

Variation Tip: You use raw honey instead of maple syrup

Nutritional Information Per Serving:

Calories 325 | Fat 17.7g | Sodium 346mg | Carbs 36.3g | Fiber 7.6g | Sugar 9.7g | Protein 9.3g

Gluten-free Broccoli Salad

Prep Time: 10 minutes

Cook Time: 5 minutes

Serves: 4

Ingredients:

- 4 cups broccoli florets, chopped
- ¼ cup walnuts, chopped
- ¼ cup artichoke hearts, drained & chopped
- 1 roasted red pepper, chopped
- ⅓ cup onion, chopped

For dressing:

- 1 tsp garlic powder
- 1 lemon juice
- 3 tbsp water
- 5 tbsp tahini
- ½ tsp salt

Preparation:

1. Add broccoli, walnuts, artichoke hearts, red pepper, and onion into the mixing bowl and mix well.
2. In a small bowl, mix all dressing ingredients and pour over salad. Toss well.

Serving Suggestion: Serve chilled

Variation Tip: If you don't have tahini, you can also use seed and nut butter

Nutritional Information Per Serving:

Calories 202 | Fat 15.1g |Sodium 387mg | Carbs 13.3g | Fiber 5.1g | Sugar 3.1g | Protein 8g

Healthy Dragon Fruit Smoothie

Prep Time: 5 minutes

Cook Time: 5 minutes

Serves: 2

Ingredients:

- ½ scoop whey protein powder
- 2 tbsp fresh lime juice
- ¾ cup unsweetened almond milk
- 2 bananas, sliced
- 1 cup mango, chopped
- 1 cup dragon fruit, cubed
- ¼ cup ice cubes

Preparation:

1. Add all ingredients into the blender and blend until smooth.

Serving Suggestion: Top with sliced lemon and mint leaves and serve

Variation Tip: Add a little honey for a sweet taste

Nutritional Information Per Serving:

Calories 200 | Fat 2.5g | Sodium 84mg | Carbs 41g | Fiber 4.8g | Sugar 25.9g | Protein 7.9g

Banana Peanut Butter Smoothie

Prep Time: 5 minutes

Cook Time: 5 minutes

Serves: 1

Ingredients:

- 1 ripe banana
- 1 tbsp peanut butter
- 1 tbsp cocoa powder
- ½ tsp vanilla
- 2 dates, pitted
- 1 cup unsweetened almond milk
- 1 cup ice cubes

Preparation:

1. Add all the ingredients into the blender and blend until smooth.

Serving Suggestion: Drizzle with chocolate sauce and serve

Variation Tip: You can use any non-dairy milk instead of almond milk

Nutritional Information Per Serving:

Calories 304 | Fat 12.7g |Sodium 263mg | Carbs 47.8g | Fiber 8g | Sugar 26.8g | Protein 7.7g

Cucumber Pineapple Salad

Prep Time: 10 minutes

Cook Time: 5 minutes

Serves: 8

Ingredients:

- 5 cups pineapple, cut into 1-inch cubes
- ½ cup cilantro, chopped
- ½ onion, sliced
- 2 cucumbers, cut into ½-inch chunks
- ¼ tsp chili powder
- 2 tbsp fresh lime juice
- 1 lime zest, grated
- ½ tsp kosher salt

Preparation:

1. Add pineapple, cilantro, onion, and cucumber into the mixing bowl and mix well.
2. In a small bowl, mix lime juice, lime zest, chili powder, and salt and pour over salad. Toss well.

Serving Suggestion: Place salad bowl in the refrigerator for 1 hour then serve chilled

Variation Tip: Add cayenne pepper for more flavor

Nutritional Information Per Serving:

Calories 66 | Fat 0.2g | Sodium 152mg | Carbs 17g | Fiber 2g | Sugar 11.7g | Protein 1.2g

Protein Packed Chickpea Salad

Prep Time: 10 minutes

Cook Time: 5 minutes

Serves: 6

Ingredients:

- 15 oz can chickpeas, drained & rinsed
- 4 oz feta cheese, diced
- ¼ cup fresh cilantro, chopped
- 1 avocado, sliced
- ½ onion, sliced
- 1 cucumber, sliced
- 1½ cups cherry tomatoes, halved
- 1 garlic clove, minced
- 3 tbsp lemon juice
- 3 tbsp olive oil
- ½ tsp sea salt

Preparation:

1. Add chickpeas, cheese, cilantro, avocado, onion, cucumber, cherry tomatoes, and garlic into the mixing bowl and mix well.

2. In a small bowl, mix olive oil, lemon juice, and salt and pour over salad. Toss well.

Serving Suggestion: Serve immediately

Variation Tip: Add some black olives into the salad

Nutritional Information Per Serving:

Calories 285 | Fat 18.6g | Sodium 586mg | Carbs 24.5g | Fiber 6.4g | Sugar 3.5g | Protein 7.8g

Mango Avocado Salad

Prep Time: 10 minutes

Cook Time: 5 minutes

Serves: 6

Ingredients:

- 1 cup cherry tomatoes, halved
- 3 tbsp onion, diced
- 2 tbsp fresh cilantro, chopped
- 1 tsp garlic, minced
- 1 lemon juice
- 4 avocado, peel & cubed
- 2 mangoes, peel & cubed
- ¾ tsp salt

Preparation:

1. Add all ingredients into the mixing bowl and toss well.

Serving Suggestion: Serve immediately

Variation Tip: You can also add grape tomatoes instead of cherry tomatoes

Nutritional Information Per Serving:

Calories 115 | Fat 3.8g |Sodium 294mg | Carbs 20.6g | Fiber 4.3g | Sugar 16.3g | Protein 2g

Tasty Baked Cabbage

Prep Time: 10 minutes

Cook Time: 25 minutes

Serves: 2

Ingredients:

- 2 lbs. cabbage, shredded
- 3 tbsp olive oil
- 1 tbsp paprika
- 1 tbsp garlic powder
- 1 tsp salt

Preparation:

1. In a large bowl, add shredded cabbage, oil, paprika, garlic powder, and salt and toss well.
2. Add cabbage mixture into the baking dish and bake at 400 degrees F for 25 minutes or until cooked through.

Serving Suggestion: Serve immediately

Variation Tip: Add your choice of seasoning

Nutritional Information Per Serving:

Calories 317 | Fat 21.9g |Sodium 1247mg | Carbs 31.3g | Fiber 13.1g | Sugar 15.9g | Protein 7g

Roasted Brussels Sprouts

Prep Time: 10 minutes

Cook Time: 20 minutes

Serves: 4

Ingredients:

- 1 lb. Brussels sprouts, trimmed & sliced in half
- 1½ tbsp olive oil
- 2 tsp paprika
- 2 tsp garlic powder
- ½ tsp salt

Preparation:

1. Add Brussels sprouts, olive oil, paprika, garlic powder, and salt into the bowl and toss well.
2. Spread Brussels sprouts onto the parchment-lined baking sheet and bake at 400 degrees F for 20 minutes. Stir halfway through.

Serving Suggestion: Serve warm

Variation Tip: Add your choice of seasonings

Nutritional Information Per Serving:

Calories 102 | Fat 5.8g |Sodium 320mg | Carbs 11.9g | Fiber 4.8g | Sugar 2.9g | Protein 4.3g

Dips and Sauces Recipes

Flavorful Tzatziki

Prep Time: 10 minutes

Cook Time: 5 minutes

Serves: 6

Ingredients:

- 1 cup cucumber, shredded & squeeze
- 1 cup unsweetened dairy-free yogurt
- ½ tsp garlic, crushed
- 1½ tbsp lemon juice
- 1 tbsp mint, minced
- 2 tbsp fresh dill, chopped
- ½ tsp salt

Preparation:

1. Add cucumber, yogurt, garlic, lemon juice, mint, dill, and salt into the bowl and mix well.
2. Cover and place in refrigerator for 15 minutes.

Serving Suggestion: Serve with pita bread

Variation Tip: You can also make this sauce using almond yogurt

Nutritional Information Per Serving:

Calories 29 | Fat 0.1g | Sodium 231mg | Carbs 4.4g | Fiber 0.3g | Sugar 3.1g | Protein 2.5g

Sun-dried Tomato Dip

Prep Time: 10 minutes

Cook Time: 5 minutes

Serves: 4

Ingredients:

- 15 oz can cannellini beans, drained
- 1 tsp oregano leaves
- ¼ cup sun-dried tomatoes
- 2 tsp lemon juice
- 3 tbsp olive oil
- 1 garlic clove, minced
- Pepper
- Salt

Preparation:

1. Add all ingredients into the food processor and process until smooth.
2. Transfer dip into a bowl and store in the refrigerator.

Serving Suggestion: Serve the dip in a bowl with crackers and vegetables

Variation Tip: Add dashes of hot sauce and a pinch of cayenne pepper for more flavor

Nutritional Information Per Serving:

Calories 193 | Fat 10.6g | Sodium 122mg | Carbs 18.2g | Fiber 8.5g | Sugar 1.2g | Protein 6.8g

Roasted Pepper Dip

Prep Time: 10 minutes.

Cook Time: 5 minutes.

Serves: 6

Ingredients:

- 1 cup roasted red peppers
- ¼ tsp cumin
- ½ tsp paprika
- 1 tbsp lemon juice
- 1 garlic clove
- ¾ cup tahini
- ½ tsp sea salt

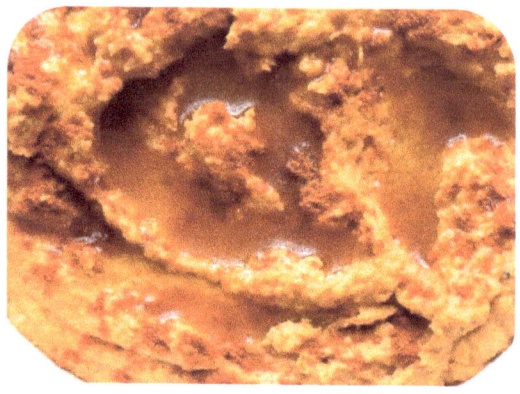

Preparation:

1. Add all ingredients into the blender and blend until smooth.

Serving Suggestion: Serve dip with vegetables

Variation tip: Add a pinch of chili flakes for more flavors

Nutritional Information Per Serving:

Calories 189 | Fat 16.3g | Sodium 264mg | Carbs 8.6g | Fiber 3.3g | Sugar 1.6g | Protein 5.5g

Easy White Bean Dip

Prep Time: 10 minutes

Cook Time: 5 minutes

Serves: 8

Ingredients:

- 30 oz can cannellini beans, rinsed & drained
- 2 tbsp fresh lemon juice
- ½ cup olive oil
- 1 tbsp garlic, minced
- 1 tsp pepper
- 1 tsp salt

Preparation:

1. Add all ingredients into the food processor and process until smooth.
2. Transfer dip to the bowl and place in refrigerator for 2 hours.

Serving Suggestion: Serve dip with vegetables

Variation Tip: You can substitute cannellini beans with another type of white beans

Nutritional Information Per Serving:

Calories 209 | Fat 12.7g |Sodium 374mg | Carbs 17.8g | Fiber 8.3g | Sugar 0.9g | Protein 6.7g

Peanut Sauce

Prep Time: 5 minutes

Cook Time: 5 minutes

Serves: 6

Ingredients:

- 1 tsp ginger, grated
- 2 garlic cloves, minced
- ½ lemon juice
- 1 tbsp soy sauce
- 1 tbsp maple syrup
- ½ cup creamy peanut butter

Preparation:

1. Add peanut butter into the microwave-safe bowl and microwave for 30 seconds
2. Add remaining ingredients into the peanut butter and stir well

Serving Suggestion: Serve sauce with noodles

Variation Tip: You can also add raw honey instead of maple syrup

Nutritional Information Per Serving:

Calories 139 | Fat 10.9g | Sodium 250mg | Carbs 7.2g | Fiber 1.4g | Sugar 4.1g | Protein 5.6g

Tahini Sauce

Prep Time: 5 minutes

Cook Time: 5 minutes

Serves: 8

Ingredients:

- ½ cup tahini
- 2 tbsp warm water
- ½ tsp Dijon mustard
- ¼ cup lemon juice
- 2 garlic cloves, minced
- ¼ tsp pepper
- ½ tsp salt

Preparation:

1. Add all ingredients into the bowl and stir until well combined.

Serving Suggestion: Drizzle sauce over vegetables and serve

Variation Tip: Add 1 teaspoon maple syrup to sweeten it a little

Nutritional Information Per Serving:

Calories 93 | Fat 8.1g |Sodium 170mg | Carbs 3.7g | Fiber 1.5g | Sugar 0.2g | Protein 2.7g

Lunch Recipes

Coconut Pumpkin Soup

Prep Time: 10 minutes

Cook Time: 30 minutes

Serves: 6

Ingredients:

- 2 cups pumpkin puree
- 1 tsp curry powder
- 2 shallots, chopped
- ½ onion, chopped
- 1 cup coconut cream
- 4 cups vegetable broth
- ½ tsp ground ginger
- 4 tbsp olive oil
- Pepper
- Salt

Preparation:

1. Heat oil in a saucepan over medium heat.
2. Add onion and shallot and sauté until softened.
3. Add ginger and curry powder and stir well.
4. Add broth, pumpkin puree, and coconut cream and stir well. Simmer for 10 minutes.
5. Puree the soup using a blender until smooth. Season with pepper and salt.

Serving Suggestion: Sprinkle pumpkin seeds on top of the soup and serve

Variation Tip: Add a teaspoon of maple syrup for a little sweetness

Nutritional Information Per Serving:

Calories 231 | Fat 20.1g | Sodium 547mg | Carbs 10.6g | Fiber 3.6g | Sugar 4.9g | Protein 5.2g

Garlic Basil Tomato Soup

Prep Time: 10 minutes

Cook Time: 5 minutes

Serves: 4

Ingredients:

- 28 oz can tomatoes, diced
- 1 tbsp dried oregano
- 1 tsp garlic, minced
- 2 tbsp olive oil
- 1 tbsp balsamic vinegar
- 1 tbsp dried basil
- Pepper
- Salt

Preparation:

1. Heat oil in a saucepan over medium heat.
2. Add garlic, basil, and oregano and sauté for 30 seconds.
3. Add tomatoes, vinegar, pepper, and salt and simmer for 3-5 minutes.

Serving Suggestion: Serve hot with crusty bread

Variation Tip: Add some chili flakes for more flavor

Nutritional Information Per Serving:

Calories 108 | Fat 7.1g | Sodium 462mg | Carbs 11.2g | Fiber 3.9g | Sugar 6.8g | Protein 2g

Cauliflower Carrot Soup

Prep Time: 10 minutes

Cook Time: 25 minutes

Serves: 8

Ingredients:

- 1 cauliflower head, chopped
- 8 cups vegetable broth
- 1 onion, diced
- 4 carrots, shredded
- ½ tsp turmeric powder
- ½ tbsp ginger, grated
- 5 oz coconut milk
- 1 tbsp olive oil
- 1 tbsp curry powder
- Pepper
- Salt

Preparation:

1. Heat oil in a saucepan over medium heat.
2. Add onion and sauté for 5 minutes. Add cauliflower, carrots, and broth and bring to boil.
3. Turn heat to medium-low and simmer until vegetables are softened.
4. Add curry powder, turmeric, and ginger and stir well.
5. Puree the soup using a blender until smooth.
6. Add coconut milk and stir well. Season with pepper and salt.

Serving Suggestion: Sprinkle some paprika on top of the soup and serve

Variation Tip: You can also add vegetable stock instead of broth

Nutritional Information Per Serving:

Calories 125 | Fat 7.5g |Sodium 817mg | Carbs 8.7g | Fiber 2.6g | Sugar 4.2g | Protein 6.5g

Cauliflower Spinach Rice

Prep Time: 10 minutes

Cook Time: 10 minutes

Serves: 4

Ingredients:

- 5 oz baby spinach
- 4 cups cauliflower rice
- ¼ tsp chili powder
- 1 tsp garlic, minced
- 3 tbsp olive oil
- 1 fresh lime juice
- ¼ cup vegetable broth
- Pepper
- Salt

Preparation:

1. Heat oil in a pan over medium heat. Add garlic and sauté for 30 seconds.
2. Add cauliflower rice, chili powder, pepper, and salt and cook for 2 minutes.
3. Add broth and lime juice and stir well.
4. Add spinach and cook until spinach is wilted.

Serving Suggestion: Serve warm

Variation Tip: You can also add some sautéed mushrooms

Nutritional Information Per Serving:

Calories 127 | Fat 10.9g | Sodium 146mg | Carbs 7g | Fiber 3.4g | Sugar 2.6g | Protein 3.4g

Basil Zucchini Noodles

Prep Time: 10 minutes

Cook Time: 10 minutes

Serves: 2

Ingredients:

- 1 zucchini, spiralized
- ¼ cup pine nuts
- ⅓ cup water
- 1¼ cup fresh basil
- ¾ cup cherry tomatoes, halved
- 1 avocado, chopped
- 2 tbsp fresh lemon juice
- Pepper
- Salt

Preparation:

1. Add zucchini noodles and tomatoes into the bowl.
2. Add remaining ingredients into the blender and blend until smooth.
3. Pour blended mixture over zucchini noodles. Toss well.

Serving Suggestion: Serve immediately.

Variation Tip: You can also add grape tomatoes instead of cherry tomatoes

Nutritional Information Per Serving:

Calories 355 | Fat 31.8g |Sodium 102mg | Carbs 17.5g | Fiber 9.6g | Sugar 5g | Protein 6.6g

Sautéed Asparagus & Mushrooms

Prep Time: 10 minutes

Cook Time: 5 minutes

Serves: 4

Ingredients:

- 1 lb. asparagus, trimmed and cut into pieces
- 3 tbsp olive oil
- 10 mushrooms, cleaned & sliced
- ¼ cup water
- Pepper
- Salt

Preparation:

1. Heat oil in a pan over medium heat.
2. Add mushroom and sauté for 1-2 minutes.
3. Transfer mushrooms onto a plate.
4. Add asparagus to the same pan and cook for 2-3 minutes.
5. Return mushrooms to the pan and stir for a minute. Season with pepper and salt.

Serving Suggestion: Serve with cooked cauliflower rice

Variation Tip: Add some chili flakes into the sautéed asparagus & mushrooms

Nutritional Information Per Serving:

Calories 122 | Fat 10.8g | Sodium 44mg | Carbs 5.9g | Fiber 2.8g | Sugar 2.9g | Protein 3.9g

Simple Eggplant Adobo

Prep Time: 10 minutes

Cook Time: 15 minutes

Serves: 6

Ingredients:

- 5 medium eggplants, cut into 2-inch pieces
- ½ cup olive oil
- 1 tbsp garlic, chopped
- 2 tbsp soy sauce
- ⅓ cup vinegar
- Pepper
- Salt

Preparation:

1. Heat oil in a pan over medium-high heat.
2. Fry eggplant pieces and drain on a paper towel. Set aside.
3. In a separate pan add soy sauce, garlic, vinegar, pepper, and salt. Bring to boil.
4. Add fried eggplant pieces into the pan and stir well to coat. Cover and cook for 3 minutes.

Serving Suggestion: Serve with cooked rice

Variation Tip: Add some roasted peanuts

Nutritional Information Per Serving:

Calories 168 | Fat 16.8g |Sodium 329mg | Carbs 5.2g | Fiber 1.8g | Sugar 2.7g | Protein 1.3g

Sautéed Spinach

Prep Time: 10 minutes

Cook Time: 5 minutes

Serves: 2

Ingredients:

- 8 oz fresh spinach, wash
- 1½ tsp sesame seeds, toasted
- 2 tsp sesame oil
- 1 tsp soy sauce
- 2 tbsp green onion, chopped
- ½ tsp garlic, minced
- Pinch of salt

Preparation:

1. Add spinach into the hot water and blanch for 30 seconds.
2. Drain spinach well and squeeze out excess liquid.
3. In mixing bowl, add green onion, oil, garlic, sesame seeds, soy sauce, and salt. Stir well.
4. Add spinach and stir to combine.

Serving Suggestion: Serve spinach with cooked rice

Variation Tip: Add some roasted crushed peanuts

Nutritional Information Per Serving:

Calories 82 | Fat 6.1g | Sodium 318mg | Carbs 5.3g | Fiber 2.9g | Sugar 0.7g | Protein 3.9g

Lemon Garlic Kale

Prep Time: 10 minutes

Cook Time: 15 minutes

Serves: 6

Ingredients:

- 1 ¾ lbs. kale, rinsed and chopped
- 1 tbsp olive oil
- 1 tbsp fresh lemon juice
- 1 tbsp garlic, minced
- 2 tbsp onion, minced
- Pepper
- Salt

Preparation:

1. Heat oil in a pan over medium-high heat.
2. Add onion and garlic and sauté for 1-2 minutes.
3. Add kale and sauté for 5 minutes. Cover and cook for 6-8 minutes.
4. Remove cover and cook for 2 minutes more.
5. Add lemon juice and stir well. Season with pepper and salt.

Serving Suggestion: Serve with cooked rice

Variation Tip: You can also add red chili flakes

Nutritional Information Per Serving:

Calories 89 | Fat 2.4g | Sodium 85mg | Carbs 14.7g | Fiber 2.1g | Sugar 0.2g | Protein 4.1g

Sautéed Veggies

Prep Time: 10 minutes

Cook Time: 7 minutes

Serves: 4

Ingredients:

- 1 squash, diced
- ½ cup mushrooms, sliced
- 1 zucchini, diced
- 2 tsp Italian seasoning
- 3 tbsp olive oil
- Pepper
- Salt

Preparation:

1. Add all zucchini, squash, mushrooms, Italian seasoning, pepper, and salt into a bowl and toss well.
2. Heat oil in a pan over medium heat.
3. Add vegetable mixture and sauté for 5-7 minutes.
4. Serve and enjoy.

Serving Suggestion: Serve with cooked brown rice

Variation Tip: Add your choice of seasoning

Nutritional Information Per Serving:

Calories 112 | Fat 11.3g |Sodium 45mg | Carbs 3.2g | Fiber 1.1g | Sugar 1.7g | Protein 1.1g

Zucchini Spinach Noodles

Prep Time: 10 minutes

Cook Time: 10 minutes

Serves: 4

Ingredients:

- 3 zucchinis, spiralized
- 1 tbsp garlic, minced
- 2 cups fresh spinach
- 2 tbsp olive oil
- Pepper
- Salt

Preparation:

1. Heat oil in a pan over medium-high heat.
2. Add garlic and sauté for 30 seconds.
3. Add spinach and zucchini noodles and cook for 2-3 minutes or until spinach is wilted. Season with pepper and salt.

Serving Suggestion: Serve warm

Variation Tip: Add ¼ cup grated vegan cheese

Nutritional Information Per Serving:

Calories 90 | Fat 7.3g | Sodium 66mg | Carbs 6.2g | Fiber 2g | Sugar 2.6g | Protein 2.3g

Spinach Broccoli Curry

Prep Time: 10 minutes

Cook Time: 30 minutes

Serves: 4

Ingredients:

- 1 cup broccoli florets
- ½ cup coconut cream
- ¼ onion, sliced
- ¼ cup olive oil
- ½ tsp ginger, minced
- ½ tsp garlic, minced
- ½ cup spinach
- 1 tbsp red curry paste
- 1½ tsp soy sauce

Preparation:

1. Heat 2 tablespoons of oil in a pan over medium-high heat.
2. Add onion and cook until softened. Add garlic and sauté for minutes.
3. Turn heat to medium-low. Add broccoli and stir well.
4. Once broccoli is cooked then set broccoli to one side of the pan.
5. Add curry paste and cook for a minute.
6. Add spinach and cook until wilted.
7. Add coconut cream, ginger, remaining oil, and soy sauce.
8. Stir well and simmer for 5 minutes.

Serving Suggestion: Serve warm with plain rice

Variation Tip: Add chili flakes for more flavor

Nutritional Information Per Serving:

Calories 206 | Fat 21g |Sodium 323mg | Carbs 5.1g | Fiber 1.5g | Sugar 1.7g | Protein 1.7g

Delicious Vegetable Curry

Prep Time: 10 minutes

Cook Time: 20 minutes

Serves: 4

Ingredients:

- 1 cup zucchini, chopped
- ½ cup vegetable stock
- 14 oz can coconut milk
- 3 tbsp green curry paste
- 1 cup green beans, cleaned & chopped
- ½ tbsp ginger, grated
- 2 tsp tamari
- 1 fresh lime juice
- 2 cups spinach
- 2 tsp olive oil
- Pinch of salt

Preparation:

1. Heat oil in a saucepan over medium heat.
2. Add ginger and sauté for 2 minutes. Add green beans, zucchini, carrots, and salt and sauté for 2-3 minutes.
3. Add curry paste and cook for 2 minutes.
4. Add coconut milk and stock and stir well.
5. Turn heat to low. Cover and simmer for 10 minutes.
6. Add spinach and stir until spinach is wilted.
7. Stir in lime juice and tamari.

Serving Suggestion: Serve with plain rice or brown rice

Variation Tip: Add chili powder for an extra spicy flavor

Nutritional Information Per Serving:

Calories 270 | Fat 25.9g |Sodium 686mg | Carbs 10.3g | Fiber 1.7g | Sugar 1g | Protein 3.7g

Stir Fried Carrots & Cabbage

Prep Time: 10 minutes

Cook Time: 10 minutes

Serves: 6

Ingredients:

- 6 cups cabbage, shredded
- 1 tbsp ginger, minced
- 1 tbsp olive oil
- ¼ cup water
- 4 cups carrots, shredded
- ½ tsp turmeric
- ½ tsp sea salt

Preparation:

1. Heat oil in a pan over medium-high heat.
2. Add cabbage and cook for 5-8 minutes.
3. Add carrots and cook for 2-3 minutes.
4. Add ginger, turmeric, water, and salt and stir well. Turn heat to low and cook until carrots are softened.

Serving Suggestion: Serve warm

Variation Tip: Add green onion once cooked

Nutritional Information Per Serving:

Calories 71 | Fat 2.5g |Sodium 220mg | Carbs 12g | Fiber 3.7g | Sugar 5.9g | Protein 1.6g

Zucchini Carrot Noodles

Prep Time: 10 minutes

Cook Time: 5 minutes

Serves: 4

Ingredients:

- 2 zucchinis, spiralized
- 2 tbsp green onion, chopped
- ½ cup red cabbage, sliced
- 1 carrot, peeled and julienned

For sauce:

- ½ cup almond butter
- 2 tbsp olive oil
- 1 lime juice
- 1 tbsp water
- 1 tbsp soy sauce
- 1 tsp fresh ginger, grated
- 1 tbsp sesame oil

Preparation:

1. In a small bowl, whisk together all the sauce ingredients.
2. In a large bowl, mix zucchini, green onion, cabbage, and carrot.
3. Pour sauce over zucchini mixture and toss well.

Serving Suggestion: Sprinkle with sesame seeds and serve

Variation Tip: Add roasted crushed peanuts

Nutritional Information Per Serving:

Calories 131 | Fat 11.8g |Sodium 248mg | Carbs 6.5g | Fiber 2g | Sugar 3g | Protein 2.2g

Dinner Recipes

Lentil Tomato Soup

Prep Time: 10 minutes

Cook Time: 30 minutes

Serves: 6

Ingredients:

- 1 cup red lentils
- 28 oz can tomatoes, diced
- 6 cups vegetable stock
- 3 medium carrots, diced
- 1 medium onion, diced
- 1 tbsp lemon juice
- 1 bay leaf
- ½ tsp ground thyme
- 1 tsp dried basil
- 1 tsp dried oregano
- 4 garlic cloves, minced

- 1 tbsp olive oil
- Pepper
- Salt

Preparation:

1. Heat oil in a pot over medium heat.
2. Add carrots, onion, and garlic and sauté for 5 minutes.
3. Add tomatoes, lentils, stock, herbs, and spices and bring to simmer for 20-25 minutes. Season soup with pepper and salt.
4. Stir in lemon juice.
5. Discard bay leaf.
6. Stir and serve.

Serving Suggestion: Serve with crusty bread

Variation Tip: You can also add Italian seasoning instead of dried herbs

Nutritional Information Per Serving:

Calories 186 | Fat 2.8g |Sodium 333mg | Carbs 31.6g | Fiber 13.4g | Sugar 7.5g | Protein 10.1g

Flavorful Quinoa Salad

Prep Time: 10 minutes

Cook Time: 20 minutes

Serves: 6

Ingredients:

- 1 cup quinoa, uncooked
- 15 oz can sweet corn
- 15 oz can black beans, rinsed
- 2 cups of water
- ¼ onion, minced
- 2 cups tomatoes, chopped

For dressing:

- ½ tsp honey
- 1 tbsp apple cider vinegar
- ⅓ cup olive oil
- ¼ cup lime juice
- ½ tsp garlic powder
- ½ tsp chili powder
- ½ tsp cumin
- 1/8 tsp paprika
- 1/8 tsp salt

Preparation:

1. Add quinoa and water into the saucepan and bring to boil.
2. Turn heat to low. Cover and simmer for 20 minutes.
3. Transfer cooked quinoa into the mixing bowl and place in the refrigerator for 2 hours.
4. In a small bowl, mix together all dressing ingredients and set aside.
5. Add onion, tomatoes, corn, and black beans into the quinoa and mix well.
6. Pour dressing over salad.
7. Stir well and serve.

Serving Suggestion: Serve with avocado slices

Variation Tip: You can also add cherry tomatoes instead of tomatoes

Nutritional Information Per Serving:

Calories 299 | Fat 13.4g | Sodium 322mg | Carbs 35.8g | Fiber 6.9g | Sugar 2.9g | Protein 9.9g

Sweet Potato Lentil Stew

Prep Time: 10 minutes

Cook Time: 35 minutes

Serves: 6

Ingredients:

- 1 large sweet potato, peeled and cubed
- ¼ tsp cumin
- 2 garlic cloves, minced
- 1 onion, diced
- 1 tbsp olive oil
- ½ tsp turmeric
- 1 bay leaf
- 6 cups vegetable broth
- 2 cups green lentils, rinsed
- Pepper
- Salt

Preparation:

1. Heat oil in a pot over medium-high heat.
2. Add garlic and onion and sauté for 3 minutes.
3. Add remaining ingredients and stir well. Bring to a boil.
4. Once boiling begins then turn heat to low and simmer for 20-30 minutes or until lentils are cooked completely.
5. Stir well and serve.

Serving Suggestion: Garnish with fresh coriander and serve

Variation Tip: Add chopped tomatoes into the stew

Nutritional Information Per Serving:

Calories 321 | Fat 4.5g |Sodium 806mg | Carbs 47.8g | Fiber 21g | Sugar 4.8g | Protein 22.3g

Quinoa Bean Chili

Prep Time: 10 minutes

Cook Time: 30 minutes

Serves: 8

Ingredients:

- 1½ cups quinoa, uncooked
- 15 oz can tomatoes, diced
- 15 oz can tomato sauce
- 15 oz can corn
- 15 oz can black beans, drained and rinsed
- 1 tbsp paprika
- 3 tbsp chili powder
- 2 tsp garlic powder
- 1 bell pepper, chopped
- 1 onion, chopped
- 4 cups of water
- 1½ tsp salt

Preparation:

1. Add all ingredients into a pot and stir everything well. Bring to boil over medium-high heat.
2. Turn heat to low and simmer for 30 minutes.
3. Stir and serve.

Serving Suggestion: Serve immediately

Variation Tip: You can also add vegetable stock instead of water

Nutritional Information Per Serving:

Calories 257 | Fat 3.4g | Sodium 1219mg | Carbs 50.4g | Fiber 9.3g | Sugar 7.9g | Protein 10.8g

Black Beans Rice

Prep Time: 10 minutes

Cook Time: 60 minutes

Serves: 6

Ingredients:

- 16 oz can black beans, rinsed
- 4 cups vegetable broth
- 1 tsp ground cumin
- 2 garlic cloves, minced
- 2 cups brown rice
- 14.5 oz canned tomatoes, diced
- ¼ tsp red pepper flakes
- 1 bell pepper, diced
- 1 onion, diced
- ¼ cup olive oil

Preparation:

1. Heat oil in a large pan over medium heat.
2. Add onion and sauté for 3-5 minutes.
3. Add bell pepper and cook for 3-5 minutes.
4. Add red pepper flakes, cumin, and garlic and sauté for a minute.
5. Add tomatoes and cook for 5 minutes.
6. Add rice and broth and stir well. Bring to a boil.
7. Cover and turn heat to low and simmer for 45 minutes.
8. Allow it to cool for 5 minutes.
9. Stir and serve.

Serving Suggestion: Serve with mushrooms frittata and crispy bacon on the side

Variation Tip: Add chopped bell pepper to the frittata

Nutritional Information Per Serving:

Calories 428 | Fat 11.5g | Sodium 938mg | Carbs 69.5g | Fiber 7.5g | Sugar 5.2g | Protein 13.2g

Spanish Rice & Beans

Prep Time: 10 minutes

Cook Time: 22 minutes

Serves: 6

Ingredients:

- 15 oz can kidney beans, drained and rinsed
- ½ cup onion, chopped
- 2 cups dry white rice
- 2 tbsp olive oil
- 1 cup salsa
- 3 cups vegetable broth
- 2 garlic cloves, minced

Preparation:

1. Heat oil in a pan over medium-high heat.
2. Add rice to the pan toast for 5-7 minutes.
3. Turn heat to medium. Add garlic and onion and sauté until softened.
4. Add broth and stir well. Cover and cook for 15 minutes.
5. Add salsa and beans and stir well.

Serving Suggestion: Sprinkle with green onions and serve

Variation Tip: Add chili powder for a spicy flavor

Nutritional Information Per Serving:

Calories 366 | Fat 6.4g |Sodium 885mg | Carbs 64.2g | Fiber 5.2g | Sugar 2.7g | Protein 11.8g

Easy Spanish Quinoa

Prep Time: 10 minutes

Cook Time: 20 minutes

Serves: 4

Ingredients:

- 1 cup quinoa
- ¼ cup onion, chopped
- 1 tsp olive oil
- 2 cups vegetable broth
- ½ cup of salsa

Preparation:

1. Heat oil in a saucepan over medium heat.
2. Add onion and sauté until tender.
3. Add quinoa, broth, and salsa and stir well. Bring to boil.
4. Turn heat to low, cover, and simmer for 20 minutes.
5. Remove saucepan from heat.
6. Allow to cool for 5 minutes.
7. Fluff quinoa with fork and serve.

Serving Suggestion: Drizzle with lemon juice and serve

Variation Tip: Add green onions to the quinoa

Nutritional Information Per Serving:

Calories 197 | Fat 4.5g |Sodium 579mg | Carbs 30.4g | Fiber 3.7g | Sugar 1.6g | Protein 9g

Healthy Lentil Rice

Prep Time: 10 minutes

Cook Time: 20 minutes

Serves: 6

Ingredients:

- 1½ cups brown rice
- ½ cup dry green lentils
- 3½ cups vegetable stock
- 2 tbsp olive oil
- 1 tsp sea salt

Preparation:

1. Add oil into an instant pot. Set the instant pot on sauté mode.
2. Add rice and sauté for 5 minutes.
3. Add remaining ingredients and stir well.
4. Cover and cook on high for 15 minutes.
5. Allow pressure to completely release before removing the lid.

Serving Suggestion: Stir well and serve immediately

Variation Tip: You can also add your choice of seasoning

Nutritional Information Per Serving:

Calories 268 | Fat 6.1g |Sodium 315mg | Carbs 45.8g | Fiber 6.5g | Sugar 0.3g | Protein 7.7g

Mushroom Garlic Quinoa

Prep Time: 10 minutes

Cook Time: 10 minutes

Serves: 2

Ingredients:

- 1 cup cooked quinoa
- 1 tbsp olive oil
- 3 garlic cloves, roasted
- 1½ cups mushrooms, sliced
- ¼ tsp pepper
- ¾ tsp salt

Preparation:

1. Heat oil in a pan over medium-high heat.
2. Add mushrooms and garlic and cook until mushrooms softened.
3. Add quinoa, pepper, and salt and stir well and cook for 1 minute.

Serving Suggestion: Garnish with parsley and serve

Variation Tip: Add a chopped tomato into the quinoa

Nutritional Information Per Serving:

Calories 392 | Fat 12.3g | Sodium 880mg | Carbs 57.9g | Fiber 6.6g | Sugar 1g | Protein 14g

Brown Rice Broccoli Casserole

Prep Time: 10 minutes

Cook Time: 40 minutes

Serves: 8

Ingredients:

- 2 cups brown rice, cooked
- 3 cups broccoli florets
- 2 garlic cloves, minced
- 1 onion, chopped
- 1 tbsp olive oil

For sauce:

- 1 garlic clove, minced
- ¼ cup nutritional yeast flakes
- 1 cup water
- 1 cup cashews
- 1 tbsp tapioca starch
- 1 tbsp onion, chopped
- 1½ tsp salt

Preparation:

1. Preheat the oven to 400 degrees F.
2. Spray a 9*13-inch casserole dish with cooking spray and set aside.
3. For the sauce: add all sauce ingredients into the blender and blend until smooth.
4. Heat oil in a pan over medium-high heat.
5. Add garlic and onion and sauté until onion is softened.
6. Add broccoli and cook for a minute.
7. Add rice and sauce and stir to combine.
8. Add broccoli rice mixture into the prepared casserole dish.
9. Cover and bake for 35-40 minutes.

Serving Suggestion: Serve warm

Variation Tip: You can also use cooked white rice instead of brown rice

Nutritional Information Per Serving:

Calories 327 | Fat 11.4g | Sodium 459mg | Carbs 49.2g | Fiber 4.6g | Sugar 2.1g | Protein 9.7g

Mushroom Barley Soup

Prep Time: 10 minutes

Cook Time: 8 hours

Serves: 8

Ingredients:

- 16 oz button mushrooms, sliced
- 2/3 cup pearl barley
- 1 large onion, diced
- 1½ tsp olive oil
- 6 cups vegetable broth
- 1 garlic clove, minced
- ¼ tsp pepper
- ½ tsp salt

Preparation:

1. Heat oil in a pan over medium-high heat.
2. Add onion and sauté for 5 minutes.
3. Add garlic and sauté for 30 seconds.
4. Add mushrooms and cook for 5 minutes.
5. Transfer onion mushroom mixture into the crockpot along with broth, barley, pepper, and salt. Stir well.
6. Cover and cook on low for 8 hours.
7. Stir and serve.

Serving Suggestion: Garnish with parsley and serve warm

Variation Tip: You can also add your choice of seasoning in the soup

Nutritional Information Per Serving:

Calories 115 | Fat 2.3g | Sodium 725mg | Carbs 17.4g | Fiber 3.6g | Sugar 2.4g | Protein 7.3g

Nutritious Lentil Stew

Prep Time: 10 minutes

Cook Time: 45 minutes

Serves: 6

Ingredients:

- 1½ cups brown lentils, rinsed
- 1 tbsp garlic, minced
- 1 onion, chopped
- ¼ tsp cayenne pepper
- 1 bay leaf
- 6 cups vegetable stock
- ½ tsp cumin
- ½ tsp paprika
- 1 tsp Italian seasoning
- 2 celery stalks, chopped
- 1 potato, diced
- 2 carrots, diced
- 14 oz canned tomatoes, diced
- ½ tsp thyme
- 1 tbsp olive oil
- Salt

Preparation:

1. Heat oil in a saucepan over medium heat.
2. Add onion and sauté for 3 minutes.
3. Add garlic and sauté for a minute.
4. Add thyme, cumin, paprika, Italian seasoning, and celery and cook for 30 seconds.
5. Add stock, bay leaf, potatoes, carrots, tomatoes, and lentils and mix well, and bring to boil.
6. Turn heat to low and simmer for 40 minutes. Remove bay leaf. Season with pepper and salt.

Serving Suggestion: Garnish with chopped coriander and serve

Variation Tip: You can also add cherry tomatoes into the stew

Nutritional Information Per Serving:

Calories 117 | Fat 4.1g | Sodium 953mg | Carbs 13.9g | Fiber 2.9g | Sugar 5.1g | Protein 6.6g

Black Bean Chili

Prep Time: 10 minutes

Cook Time: 60 minutes

Serves: 4

Ingredients:

- 30 oz canned black beans, drained and rinsed
- ¼ cup tomato paste
- ½ cup vegetable broth
- 1 cup water
- 28 oz canned tomatoes, diced
- 1½ cups corn
- ¼ tsp cayenne pepper
- ½ tsp paprika
- 1½ tsp ground cumin
- 1 tbsp coconut sugar
- 2½ tbsp chili powder
- 2 carrots, peeled and chopped
- 2 sweet potatoes, cubed
- 1 tbsp olive oil
- 1 tbsp garlic, minced
- 1 onion, diced
- ¼ tsp pepper
- ½ tsp salt

Preparation:

1. Heat oil in a pot over medium heat.
2. Add garlic and onion and sauté for 2-3 minutes.
3. Add remaining ingredients and stir to combine. Bring to a boil.
4. Turn heat to medium-low and simmer for 60 minutes.
5. Stir well and serve.

Serving Suggestion: Garnish with chopped coriander and serve

Variation Tip: If you don't have canned beans then you can use soaked & cooked beans

Nutritional Information Per Serving:

Calories 382 | Fat 6.3g | Sodium 1691mg | Carbs 71.3g | Fiber 18.7g | Sugar 15.5g | Protein 17.9g

Barley Spinach Risotto

Prep Time: 10 minutes

Cook Time: 6 hours

Serves: 4

Ingredients:

- 1 cup pearl barley
- 2 garlic cloves, chopped
- 1 onion, chopped
- 2½ cups fresh spinach, chopped
- 2½ cups vegetable stock
- Pepper
- Salt

Preparation:

1. Add barley, vegetable stock, garlic, and onion to a crockpot and stir well.
2. Cover and cook on low for 6 hours.
3. Add spinach and stir well. Season with pepper and salt.

Serving Suggestion: Garnish with parsley and serve

Variation Tip: Add sliced mushrooms into the risotto

Nutritional Information Per Serving:

Calories 194 | Fat 0.7g | Sodium 59mg | Carbs 42.6g | Fiber 8.8g | Sugar 1.7g | Protein 5.9g

Delicious Pumpkin Risotto

Prep Time: 10 minutes

Cook Time: 1 hour 30 minutes

Serves: 4

Ingredients:

- 1½ cup Arborio rice
- 2 cups roasted pumpkin
- 1 tsp black pepper
- 4 cups vegetable broth
- ½ cup onion, chopped
- 1 tbsp garlic, crushed
- 2 tsp dried sage
- 2 tbsp olive oil
- 2 tsp salt

Preparation:

1. Add oil into the instant pot. Set instant pot on sauté mode.
2. Add onion, garlic, and sage and sauté until onion is softened.
3. Add remaining ingredients and stir well.
4. Cover pot with a lid. Cook on slow cook mode for 1½ hours.
5. Stir well and serve.

Serving Suggestion: Garnish with grated vegan cheese and serve

Variation Tip: Add some sautéed mushrooms

Nutritional Information Per Serving:

Calories 509 | Fat 15g | Sodium 2116mg | Carbs 77.4g | Fiber 2.6g | Sugar 1.3g | Protein 15.9g

Desserts Recipes

Chia Chocó Pudding

Prep Time: 10 minutes

Cook Time: 10 minutes

Serves: 3

Ingredients:

- 14 oz canned coconut milk
- ½ cup maple syrup
- ½ cup of cocoa powder
- 1 tsp vanilla
- ¼ cup chia seeds
- Pinch of salt

Preparation:

1. Add all ingredients into the blender and blend until smooth.
2. Pour pudding mixture into the serving cups and place in the refrigerator for 6 hours.

Serving Suggestion: Serve chilled

Variation Tip: Add chopped nuts

Nutritional Information Per Serving:

Calories 480 | Fat 33.3g |Sodium 75mg | Carbs 49g | Fiber 4.3g | Sugar 31.7g | Protein 7.3g

Choco Peanut Butter Muffins

Prep Time: 10 minutes

Cook Time: 20 minutes

Serves: 12

Ingredients:

- 1 cup peanut butter
- ½ cup of cocoa powder
- 1 cup applesauce
- 1 tsp baking soda
- 1 tsp vanilla
- ½ cup maple syrup

Preparation:

1. Preheat the oven to 350 degrees F.
2. Add all the ingredients into the blender and blend until smooth.
3. Pour blended mixture into the 12 silicone muffin molds.
4. Bake in preheated oven for 20 minutes.
5. Serve and enjoy.

Serving Suggestion: Allow to cool completely then serve

Variation Tip: Add chocolate chips into the mixture

Nutritional Information Per Serving:

Calories 178 | Fat 11.3g | Sodium 205mg | Carbs 17.3g | Fiber 2.6g | Sugar 12g | Protein 6.1g

Quick Kiwi Popsicle

Prep Time: 5 minutes

Cook Time: 5 minutes

Serves: 4

Ingredients:

- 4 kiwis, peel and cut into chunks
- ¼ cup of sugar
- ¼ cup of water

Preparation:

1. Add all the ingredients into a blender and blend until smooth.
2. Pour blended mixture into popsicle molds and place in refrigerator until set.

Serving Suggestion: Serve chilled

Variation Tip: Add some fresh berries along with the kiwi

Nutritional Information Per Serving:

Calories 93 | Fat 0.4g |Sodium 3mg | Carbs 23.6g | Fiber 2.3g | Sugar 19.3g | Protein 0.9g

Baked Apple

Prep Time: 10 minutes

Cook Time: 30 minutes

Serves: 6

Ingredients:

- 2 apples, peel, core, and slice
- ¼ cup brown sugar
- 1 tsp cinnamon
- ¼ cup of sugar
- ¼ tsp salt

Preparation:

1. Preheat the oven to 350 degrees F.
2. Spray a 9-inch round baking dish with cooking spray and set aside.
3. Add cinnamon, brown sugar, sugar, and salt into the zip-lock bag and mix well.
4. Add apple slices into the bag and shake until well coated.
5. Add apple slices into the prepared baking dish.
6. Bake for 25-30 minutes.

Serving Suggestion: Serve with vegan vanilla ice cream

Variation Tip: You can also add apple pie spice instead of cinnamon

Nutritional Information Per Serving:

Calories 94 | Fat 0.1g | Sodium 99mg | Carbs 24.8g | Fiber 2g | Sugar 21.9g | Protein 0.2g

Easy Lemon Popsicles

Prep Time: 5 minutes

Cook Time: 5 minutes

Serves: 10

Ingredients:

- 1 cup fresh lemon juice
- 2 cups of water
- 5 drops liquid stevia

Preparation:

1. Mix together water, lemon juice, and liquid stevia and pour into the popsicle molds.
2. Place in refrigerator for 6 hours or until set.

Serving Suggestion: Serve chilled

Variation Tip: You can also add maple syrup or honey instead of stevia

Nutritional Information Per Serving:

Calories 6 | Fat 0.2g | Sodium 6mg | Carbs 0.5g | Fiber 0.1g | Sugar 0.5g | Protein 0.2g

Easy Strawberry Sorbet

Prep Time: 5 minutes

Cook Time: 5 minutes

Serves: 6

Ingredients:

- 16 oz frozen strawberries
- 2 tbsp honey
- ¼ cup warm water

Preparation:

1. Add frozen strawberries into the blender and blend until smooth.
2. Add warm water and honey and blend until smooth.
3. Pour blended strawberry mixture into the container and place in the freezer for 2 hours.

Serving Suggestion: Garnish with mint leaves and serve

Variation Tip: Add lemon juice to the strawberry sorbet

Nutritional Information Per Serving:

Calories 46 | Fat 0g |Sodium 1mg | Carbs 12.3g | Fiber 1.5g | Sugar 10.2g | Protein 0g

Blueberry Popsicles

Prep Time: 5 minutes

Cook Time: 5 minutes

Serves: 8

Ingredients:

- 3 cups frozen blueberries
- 2 tbsp fresh lemon juice
- ¼ cup honey

Preparation:

1. Add all the ingredients into the blender and blend until smooth.
2. Pour blended mixture into the popsicle molds and place in refrigerator 6 hours or until set.

Serving Suggestion: Serve with some fresh blueberries

Variation Tip: You can also add maple syrup instead of honey

Nutritional Information Per Serving:

Calories 64 | Fat 0.2g |Sodium 2mg | Carbs 16.7g | Fiber 1.4g | Sugar 14.2g | Protein 0.5g

Strawberry Cobbler

Prep Time: 10 minutes

Cook Time: 45 minutes

Serves: 6

Ingredients:

- 2 cups strawberries, diced
- 1 cup unsweetened almond milk
- 1 cup self-rising flour
- 1¼ cup sugar
- 1 tsp vanilla essence
- ½ cup coconut oil, melted

Preparation:

1. Preheat the oven to 350 degrees F.
2. Spray 11*8-inch baking dish with cooking spray and set aside.
3. In a bowl, mix together flour and 1 cup sugar.
4. Add milk and whisk until smooth. Add vanilla essence and melted oil and mix well.
5. Pour mixture into the prepared baking dish. Sprinkle with strawberries and remaining sugar.
6. Bake for 45 minutes.

Serving Suggestion: Serve with vegan vanilla ice cream

Variation Tip: You also use any plant-based milk instead of almond milk

Nutritional Information Per Serving:

Calories 413 | Fat 19.1g | Sodium 31mg | Carbs 61.7g | Fiber 1.7g | Sugar 44.2g | Protein 2.6g

Chocolate Brownies

Prep Time: 10 minutes

Cook Time: 20 minutes

Serves: 16

Ingredients:

- 1⅓ cups all-purpose flour
- ½ tsp baking powder
- ⅓ cup cocoa powder
- 1 cup sugar
- ½ tsp vanilla
- ½ cup vegetable oil
- ½ cup water
- ½ tsp salt

Preparation:

1. Spray 8*8-inch baking pan with cooking spray and set aside.
2. In a large bowl, mix together flour, baking powder, cocoa powder, sugar, and salt.
3. In a small bowl, whisk together oil, water, and vanilla.
4. Pour the oil mixture into the flour mixture and mix until well combined.
5. Pour batter into the prepared baking pan.
6. Bake at 350 degrees F for 20 minutes.

Serving Suggestion: Serve brownies with vanilla ice cream

Variation Tip: You can also add chopped walnuts or cashews to the brownie mix

Nutritional Information Per Serving:

Calories 150 | Fat 7.1g | Sodium 75mg | Carbs 21.5g | Fiber 0.8g | Sugar 12.6g | Protein 1.4g

Lemon Cupcakes

Prep Time: 10 minutes

Cook Time: 15 minutes

Serves: 6

Ingredients:

- 1 egg
- 1 cup flour
- ½ tsp vanilla
- ½ cup unsweetened almond milk
- 2 tbsp canola oil
- ¼ tsp baking soda
- 1 tsp lemon zest, grated
- ½ cup sugar
- ¾ tsp baking powder
- ½ tsp salt

Preparation:

1. Line muffin pan with cupcake liners and set aside.
2. In a bowl, whisk egg, vanilla, almond milk, oil, and sugar until creamy.
3. Add remaining ingredients and stir until well combined.
4. Pour batter into the prepared muffin pan.
5. Bake at 350 degrees F for 15 minutes.

Serving Suggestion: Allow to cool completely then serve

Variation Tip: You can also add some lemon juice with lemon zest

Nutritional Information Per Serving:

Calories 195 | Fat 5.9g | Sodium 272mg | Carbs 33.2g | Fiber 0.7g | Sugar 16.9g | Protein 3.2g

30-Day Meal Plan

Day 1

- Breakfast- Delicious Baked Oatmeal
- Lunch- Corn Black Bean Avocado Salad
- Dinner- Lentil Tomato Soup

Day 2

- Breakfast- Perfect Vegetable Frittata
- Lunch- Gluten-free Broccoli Salad
- Dinner- Flavorful Quinoa Salad

Day 3

- Breakfast- Spinach Tomato Tofu Scramble
- Lunch- Coconut Pumpkin Soup
- Dinner- Sweet Potato Lentil Stew

Day 4

- Breakfast- Breakfast Potatoes
- Lunch- Garlic Basil Tomato Soup
- Dinner- Quinoa Bean Chili

Day 5

- Breakfast- Banana Peanut Butter Oatmeal
- Lunch- Cauliflower Carrot Soup
- Dinner- Black Beans Rice

Day 6

- Breakfast- Healthy Pumpkin Oatmeal
- Lunch- Cauliflower Spinach Rice
- Dinner- Spanish Rice & Beans

Day 7

- Breakfast- Chia Blackberry Pudding
- Lunch- Basil Zucchini Noodles
- Dinner- Easy Spanish Quinoa

Day 8

- Breakfast- Quinoa Rice Pudding
- Lunch- Sautéed Asparagus & Mushrooms
- Dinner- Healthy Lentil Rice

Day 9

- Breakfast- Sweet Chia Mango Pudding
- Lunch- Sautéed Veggies
- Dinner- Mushroom Garlic Quinoa

Day 10

- Breakfast- Pumpkin Quinoa Porridge
- Lunch- Zucchini Spinach Noodles
- Dinner- Brown Rice Broccoli Casserole

Day 11

- Breakfast- Delicious Baked Oatmeal
- Lunch- Spinach Broccoli Curry
- Dinner- Mushroom Barley Soup

Day 12

- Breakfast- Perfect Vegetable Frittata
- Lunch- Delicious Vegetable Curry
- Dinner- Nutritious Lentil Stew

Day 13

- Breakfast- Spinach Tomato Tofu Scramble
- Lunch- Zucchini Carrot Noodles
- Dinner- Black Bean Chili

Day 14

- Breakfast- Banana Peanut Butter Oatmeal
- Lunch- Roasted Brussels Sprouts
- Dinner- Barley Spinach Risotto

Day 15

- Breakfast- Banana Peanut Butter Oatmeal
- Lunch- Protein Packed Chickpea Salad
- Dinner- Delicious Pumpkin Risotto

Day 16

- Breakfast- Delicious Baked Oatmeal
- Lunch- Corn Black Bean Avocado Salad
- Dinner- Lentil Tomato Soup

Day 17

- Breakfast- Perfect Vegetable Frittata
- Lunch- Gluten-free Broccoli Salad
- Dinner- Flavorful Quinoa Salad

Day 18

- Breakfast- Spinach Tomato Tofu Scramble
- Lunch- Coconut Pumpkin Soup
- Dinner- Sweet Potato Lentil Stew

Day 19

- Breakfast- Breakfast Potatoes
- Lunch- Garlic Basil Tomato Soup
- Dinner- Quinoa Bean Chili

Day 20

- Breakfast- Banana Peanut Butter Oatmeal
- Lunch- Cauliflower Carrot Soup
- Dinner- Black Beans Rice

Day 21

- Breakfast- Healthy Pumpkin Oatmeal
- Lunch- Cauliflower Spinach Rice
- Dinner- Spanish Rice & Beans

Day 22

- Breakfast- Chia Blackberry Pudding
- Lunch- Basil Zucchini Noodles
- Dinner- Easy Spanish Quinoa

Day 23

- Breakfast- Quinoa Rice Pudding
- Lunch- Sautéed Asparagus & Mushrooms
- Dinner- Healthy Lentil Rice

Day 24

- Breakfast- Sweet Chia Mango Pudding
- Lunch- Sautéed Veggies
- Dinner- Mushroom Garlic Quinoa

Day 25

- Breakfast- Pumpkin Quinoa Porridge
- Lunch- Zucchini Spinach Noodles
- Dinner- Brown Rice Broccoli Casserole

Day 26

- Breakfast- Delicious Baked Oatmeal
- Lunch- Spinach Broccoli Curry
- Dinner- Mushroom Barley Soup

Day 27

- Breakfast- Perfect Vegetable Frittata
- Lunch- Delicious Vegetable Curry
- Dinner- Nutritious Lentil Stew

Day 28

- Breakfast- Spinach Tomato Tofu Scramble
- Lunch- Zucchini Carrot Noodles
- Dinner- Black Bean Chili

Day 29

- Breakfast- Banana Peanut Butter Oatmeal
- Lunch- Roasted Brussels Sprouts
- Dinner- Barley Spinach Risotto

Day 30

- Breakfast- Banana Peanut Butter Oatmeal
- Lunch- Protein Packed Chickpea Salad
- Dinner- Delicious Pumpkin Risotto

Conclusion

Eating more plant-based foods and eliminating animal products from your daily diet will come with many health benefits and helps to lower the risk of heart disease, weight loss, improves physical as well as mental health, maintain blood pressure, and also control type-2 diabetes. When people want to switch to a plant-based diet, there is a variety of food and recipes are available in this category.

A plant-based diet includes minimally processed foods like whole grain, fruits, vegetables, nuts, seeds, legumes, spices, and herbs. While following the plant-based diet you have to completely avoid animal and dairy products from your diet. Nowadays most restaurants add a plant-based food menu item, most supermarkets stock alternative options for meat and dairy like cashew milk instead of cow milk, shredded jackfruit instead of pulled pork, tofu scramble instead of eggs. Following a vegan diet is one of the great opportunities to learn more about cooking and nutrition. Plant based foods are rich in fibre and also packed with vitamins, minerals, and antioxidants to keep you physically as well as mentally strong.

© Copyright 2021 - All rights reserved

The content contained within this book may not be reproduced, duplicated or transmitted without direct written permission from the author or the publisher.

Under no circumstances will any blame or legal responsibility be held against the publisher, or author, for any damages, reparation, or monetary loss due to the information contained within this book, either directly or indirectly.

Legal Notice:

This book is copyright protected. It is only for personal use. You cannot amend, distribute, sell, use, quote or paraphrase any part, or the content within this book, without the consent of the author or publisher.

Disclaimer Notice:

Please note the information contained within this document is for educational and entertainment purposes only. All effort has been executed to present accurate, up to date, reliable, complete information. No warranties of any kind are declared or implied. Readers acknowledge that the author is not engaged in the rendering of legal, financial, medical or professional advice. The content within this book has been derived from various sources. Please consult a licensed professional before attempting any techniques outlined in this book.

By reading this document, the reader agrees that under no circumstances is the author responsible for any losses, direct or indirect, that are incurred as a result of the use of the information contained within this document, including, but not limited to, errors, omissions, or inaccuracies.

www.ingramcontent.com/pod-product-compliance
Lightning Source LLC
Chambersburg PA
CBHW080608170426

43209CB00007B/1371